USBORNE BEGINNERS

VOLCANOES

Stephanie Turnbull

Designed by Nancy Leschnikoff

Illustrated by Andy Tudor

Volcano consultant: Professor Gillian Foulger,
Department of Earth Sciences, University of Durham
Reading consultant: Alison Kelly, Roehampton University
Additional illustrations by Tim Haggerty

SCHOLASTIC INC.

New York Toronto London Auckland Sydney
Mexico City New Delhi Hong Kong Buenos Aires

Contents

Exploding Earth

There are thousands of volcanoes around the world. Some spray red-hot melted rock called lava. Others blast out clouds of ash.

This is Mount Etna on Sicily shooting out lava.

A volcano forms

The Earth has an outer shell called the crust. Underneath this is a thick layer of hot rock called the mantle.

Mantle

Crust

Core

The middle of the Earth is called the core. It is made of extremely hot metal.

There are cracks in the crust. Hot rock melts and pushes up into the cracks.

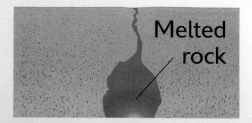

Melted rock

The melted rock builds up and bursts out as lava. This is called an eruption.

The lava hardens into rock. Layers of lava build up after many eruptions.

Volcanoes are named after Vulcan, the Roman god of fire.

Fiery fountains

Some lava is runny, so gas
inside it bubbles out easily.
This creates gentle eruptions.

This is Piton de la Fournaise,
on the island of Réunion.
Runny lava sprays out
of it like a fountain.

Runny lava is like thin honey or hot wax.
It gushes down the sides of the volcano.

The lava spreads a long way before
it cools and hardens.

A volcano with gently sloping
sides slowly builds up.

The tallest lava
fountain ever was five
times higher than the
Eiffel Tower in Paris.

Big blasts

Some volcanoes have thick lava that is full of gas bubbles. The gas makes lava burst out in a violent eruption.

Clouds of ash and big lumps of lava blast into the air.

Some lumps of lava are jagged rocks called blocks.

Other lumps cool into long, twisted shapes called bombs.

Some blocks of lava are as big as trucks.

Red-hot rivers

Lava that flows from an erupting volcano is much, much hotter than boiling water.

This glowing lava river sets fire to all the trees, plants and buildings it reaches.

Thick lava moves slowly, which gives people and animals time to escape.

Thick lava breaks
into rough chunks
as it cools down.

Runny lava sets
into smooth, swirly
shapes instead.

Deadly clouds

Violent eruptions throw out thick clouds of ash, rocks and gas. These clouds sweep down the volcano's slopes.

This terrifying ash cloud came from Mount Pinatubo in the Philippines in 1991. It covered the land all around with a thick blanket of ash.

Sometimes snow and ice on top of high volcanoes melt and mix with the hot ash.

The muddy mixture gushes down the volcano like a river of hot, wet concrete.

Clouds of ash, rocks and gas move faster than a racing car.

Undersea eruptions

Many volcanoes form under the sea.
They erupt gently and lava cools quickly
in the water.

1. An underwater
volcano grows taller
as it keeps erupting.

2. When it reaches
the water's surface,
clouds of steam rise.

3. Soon the top of
the volcano sticks
up out of the sea.

4. The lava keeps
building up and
forms an island.

This photograph taken from space shows the island of Hawaii.

Hawaii was formed by underwater volcanoes.

The dark area in the middle of the island is Mauna Loa, the world's biggest volcano.

Underwater lava can harden into round rocks called pillow lava.

Hot water

The melted rock underneath a volcano heats up the ground around it.

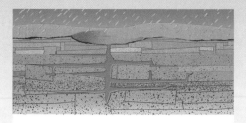 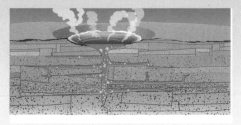

The hot ground also heats up any rain that soaks into it.

Heated water bubbles out and forms a hot spring.

In Iceland, hot spring water is used in swimming pools.

These snow monkeys are keeping warm in a steaming hot spring. The spring is high in the mountains of Japan and is heated by the Shiga Kogen volcano.

Black smokers

Hot springs called black smokers can form around underwater volcanoes.

Black smokers are jets of dark, cloudy water.

Tiny grains in the water build up to form tall chimneys.

Tubeworms and shrimps feed on the cloudy water around black smokers.

Crabs and long fish called eelpouts also live there, eating smaller animals.

Sometimes a deep sea octopus visits black smokers to search for food.

Some springs blow out pale clouds of water. They are called white smokers.

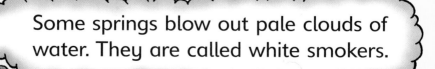

Great geysers

Sometimes water heated by a volcano shoots out of the ground with a cloud of steam. This is called a geyser.

Here you can see Old Faithful Geyser in Yellowstone National Park, USA.

Boiling water blasts out of the ground every hour.

1. Rainwater gets trapped in lots of tiny cracks in the ground.

2. Hot volcanic rock heats the water until it fizzes and boils.

3. The boiling water bursts out into the air with a whoosh.

4. It soaks back into the cracks and starts to heat up again.

Some people use hot mud from around geysers to keep their skin soft.

Dead or alive?

Volcanoes that are erupting or could erupt in the future are alive. Ones that will never erupt again are dead or extinct.

This is Mount Popa, an extinct volcano in Burma. A temple stands on the top.

A volcano can become extinct if hard lava plugs its main tube or vent.

Over many years the volcano's sides wear away, leaving the lava plug.

Some volcanoes don't erupt for thousands of years, but they are not dead – only sleeping.

Violent Vesuvius

One of the worst eruptions ever was that of Mount Vesuvius in Italy, 2,000 years ago.

Ash and rocks from the volcano rained down on a nearby town called Pompeii.

Some people hurried away from the town, but others hid in their homes instead.

Later that day, Pompeii was buried in a river of mud and ash that set hard, like cement.

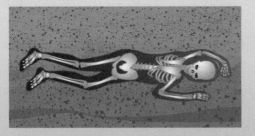

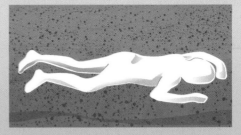

Years later, experts found holes in the rock left by bodies that rotted away.

They filled the holes with plaster, then cut away the rock to see the body shapes.

This is a plaster model of a man who was choked to death by ash.

Experts also found an oven with ancient loaves of bread inside.

American eruption

In 1980, the high, snow-covered peak of Mount St. Helens in the USA was blasted away in an enormous eruption.

This is what Mount St. Helens looked like in the years before it erupted.

Then one side of the volcano began to swell up and the ground shook.

Suddenly the volcano's side exploded in a cloud of ash and rocks.

Many small animals escaped the eruption by hiding underground.

This is how Mount St. Helens looked after the eruption. Part of the volcano was gone, and the land around was destroyed.

The volcano began rumbling again in 2004. Another eruption may be on the way.

Volcano experts

Volcanologists are people who study volcanoes and predict when they will erupt.

This volcanologist is using a machine that senses changes in ground level.

A bulge on a volcano's slope could mean melted rock is pushing up inside.

A volcano may give off lots of gas before it erupts, so experts take gas samples.

The ground may also shake before an eruption. A machine records this shaking.

Photographs taken by satellites in space show any changes in the volcano's shape.

Some people think that animals can sense when a volcano is about to erupt.

Glossary of volcano words

Here are some of the words in this book you might not know. This page tells you what they mean.

 lava - melted rock that has erupted from a volcano.

 spring - water that flows out of the ground.

 tubeworm - a long, red-tipped worm that attaches itself to the sea floor.

 geyser - a spring that shoots a jet of steaming hot water out of the ground.

 extinct - dead. An extinct volcano is one that will never erupt again.

 volcanologist - a scientist who studies volcanoes.

 satellite - a machine in space that takes pictures of the Earth's surface.

Websites to visit

If you have a computer, you can find out more about volcanoes on the Internet. On the Usborne Quicklinks website there are links to four fun websites.

Website 1 - Watch short video clips of volcanoes erupting.

Website 2 - Explore an underwater spring.

Website 3 - Try a volcano quiz.

Website 4 - Play a movie to find out more about how volcanoes form.

To visit these websites, go to **www.usborne-quicklinks.com** and type the keywords "beginners volcanoes". Then click on the link for the website you want to visit. Before you use the Internet, look at the safety guidelines inside the back cover of this book and ask an adult to read them with you.

This is Mount Etna, the largest volcano in Europe.

Index

Acknowledgements

Photographic manipulation by Mike Wheatley, Nick Wakeford and John Russell
With thanks to Rosie Dickins and Catriona Clarke

Photo credits

The publishers are grateful to the following for permission to reproduce material:
© **Age Fotostock/Powerstock** 6-7; © **Corbis** 12-13 (Alberto Garcia), 22-23 (Christophe Loviny), 25 (Roger Ressmeyer); © **Getty Images** Cover (Ezio Geneletti), 1 (Richard A Cooke III), 31 (Art Wolfe); © **Mauritius/Powerstock** 8-9; © **NASA/Science Photo Library** 15; © **National Geographic/Getty Images** 20-21 (Norbert Rosing); © **PhotoLink/Getty Images** 27; © **Reuters/Corbis** 10-11 (Tony Gentile); © **Science Photo Library** 16-17 (Akira Uchiyama); © **Still Pictures** 2-3 (Otto Hahn); © **University of Victoria** 18 (Dr Verena Tunnicliffe); © **USGS** 28-29 (Mike Poland).

Every effort has been made to trace and acknowledge ownership of copyright. If any rights have been omitted, the publishers offer to rectify this in any subsequent editions following notification.